CONTENTS

RULES 4

INTRODUCTION 6

PEOPLE 7

PLACES 57

THINGS 107

RULES

For 1 or more players!

OBJECT

▶ The object of the game is to show off your smarts by correctly identifying 10 well-known mystery topics through a series of clues.

STARTING THE GAME

▶ The youngest player spins the spinner and says, "I am a _____" (Person, Place or Thing) as shown on the spinner. The youngest player then becomes that Person, Place or Thing for the entire first round of play. This player acts solely as the reader and may not play until someone guesses correctly.

GETTING A CLUE

▶ The Reader must now flip to the start of the determined category (i.e. Person, Place or Thing) and read clue #1 aloud to the group.

▶ After listening to the clue, the player to the Reader's left (a.k.a. the Guesser) has 10 seconds to guess who the Reader is. (Players may only guess when it's their turn.)

▶ If the Guesser guesses correctly, s/he scores one point. The player to the Reader's right becomes the new Reader.

▶ If the Guesser guesses incorrectly, the player to his/her left gets the next clue and may then try to crack the 20 Questions case.

▶ Once all players have acted as the Reader, it is time to spin again! The player to the left of the last person to spin now spins to determine the type of category to be played. S/he is the first Reader for this round.

▶ Tip: Even if it sounds silly, just say it. There is no penalty for an incorrect guess! And statistics show that you have no chance of winning if you don't make a guess.

WINNING THE GAME

▶ The first player to score 10 points wins the game!

PLAYING ON YOUR OWN

▶ You get to be the Reader and the Guesser! Keep track of how many clues it takes to guess the correct answer. Get eight topics correct in less than 80 clues and you're a winner!

INTRODUCTION

Hi!

Have you ever picked up a book and found that you couldn't put it down until you finished reading it cover to cover? Boring, I'd say. Well, I promise that **20 Questions for Kids** isn't one of those all-consuming books. I have created **20 Questions for Kids** to be the type of book that can be read for ten minutes or two hours and picked up again and again. It has 1400 clues and covers more than 70 mystery topics, which should be familiar to almost all eight, nine and ten-year-old readers who haven't been hiding under a rock. The real trick is not just to guess the person, place or thing, but to guess as quickly as possible.

Every topic in the book is guaranteed to please and perplex, and has been kid-tested in my very own family lab (a.k.a. my living room). Here's how the testing works:

1. I enter the front door and my family barrages me with questions like "Guess who I am?" "Guess what I did?" and "Guess where I went today?"
2. I guess and guess and guess.
3. I hope that it will end and that I can sit down and have a cold beer.
4. My three daughters finally fill me in on the excitement in their lives.

Then I ask the girls to play my version of **20 Questions for Kids**, hoping to confound them. Alas, my plot rarely works. No beer and no time to relax, for by the fifth clue the kids have figured out my conundrum and I am back to guessing about their exciting day. However, you can benefit from trying the puzzlers in this book and seeing if you can decipher the person, place or thing on each page as fast as the Moog kids.

Either way (fast or not so fast) have fun learning and playing!

—Bob

PEOPLE

I AM A PERSON

1. I went from a successful movie career to an equally successful TV career.
2. I first achieved fame in 1935 in a series of short films.
3. I have four legs, but walk on two.
4. I'm not too smart.
5. I'm plump.
6. I'm an expert on Bugs, but I'm not an entomologist.
7. I am an animal.
8. Look out! I wear shirts but no pants.
9. My girlfriend is Petunia.
10. I have straight hair and a curly tail.
11. I'm p-p-p-p-p-porcine.
12. I am a cartoon character.
13. My stutter is often imitated.
14. I don't like to be called "the other white meat."
15. I end a lot of Warner Brothers cartoons.
16. My first and last names start with the same letter.
17. You won't find me in a sty.
18. My goodbye is, "That's All Folks."
19. I know Elmer Fudd and Yosemite Sam.
20. I don't eat that much, but I've been called a pig.

1

PEOPLE

I AM PORKY PIG

I AM A PERSON

1. I am in the movies.
2. My sister was murdered.
3. I wore black before it was fashionable.
4. My alter ego is named Miss Gulch.
5. I can fly.
6. I can cast a spell.
7. Margaret Hamilton played me in the movies.
8. People dress up like me on Halloween.
9. L. Frank Baum wrote books about me.
10. Winged monkeys do my bidding.
11. I like to frighten everyone.
12. There are three W's in my name.
13. Water makes me melt.
14. My broom does more than sweep.
15. I'm green.
16. If I was good, my name might be Glenda.
17. Dorothy stole my broom.
18. I am the author of "Surrender Dorothy."
19. To me, East is least and West is best.
20. I live near the Land of Oz.

2

PEOPLE

I AM THE WICKED WITCH OF THE WEST

I AM A PERSON

1. I died in 1968.
2. I am female.
3. Patty Duke played me in a movie.
4. My first famous word was "wah-wah," which meant "water."
5. I became blind and deaf at age two.
6. Alexander Graham Bell helped me find a teacher.
7. I learned to read Braille.
8. Annie Sullivan was my teacher.
9. I spent my life lecturing to benefit the handicapped.
10. I graduated from Radcliffe College.
11. I was the first person to earn a Bachelor of Arts degree with my challenges.
12. The award winning play "The Miracle Worker" is my story.
13. I was born with eyesight and hearing.
14. I am an author.
15. I wrote *The Story of My Life*.
16. I received the Presidential Medal of Freedom in 1964.
17. I came from Alabama.
18. When I was young, I screamed and threw terrible tantrums.
19. I became a famous lecturer.
20. I lived in the 20th century.

3

PEOPLE

I AM HELEN KELLER

I AM A PERSON

1. America first saw me in the 1960s.
2. I have one daughter and no sons.
3. I am a fictional character.
4. My job is the pits.
5. Bowling is my favorite sport.
6. I'm a member of the Water Buffalo Lodge.
7. My world is full of historical anachronisms.
8. My car doesn't use gas.
9. My fences are made of stone.
10. Everyone I know wears animal fur.
11. I started on prime time TV.
12. William Hanna and Joseph Barbera created me.
13. Alan Reed is my voice.
14. Mr. Slate is my boss.
15. My daughter wears a bone in her hair.
16. Barney is my neighbor.
17. I have my own vitamins and cereal.
18. Brontosaurus burgers are my favorite food.
19. My first name and last name start with the same letter.
20. John Goodman played me in the movies.

4

PEOPLE

I AM FRED FLINTSONE

I AM A PERSON

1. I am male.
2. I was born in 1962.
3. I dropped out of high school to pursue my dream.
4. I got my start at Yuk Yuk Comedy Club in Toronto.
5. My first TV series was *The Duck Factory* in 1983.
6. Drew and Mariah spell their last name differently than I do.
7. I'm one of the highest-paid actors in Hollywood.
8. I've been called a joker, but I played a Riddler.
9. I am Canadian.
10. I've been called a liar.
11. My second wife played an officer on *Picket Fences*.
12. REM sang the theme song to my 1999 biographical film.
13. I have co-starred with Jeff Daniels, Jeff Goldblum and Danny DeVito.
14. My physical comedy reminds some of Jerry Lewis.
15. People aren't sure if I am dumb, dumber or dumbest.
16. I dated Nurse Betty in 2000.
17. I like Christmas, but in 2000 I was a real Grinch.
18. I starred as me, myself and Irene in a 2000 Farrelly Brothers film.
19. I was America's first pet detective.
20. Some think I am a comedic genius.

5

PEOPLE

I AM JIM CARREY

I AM A PERSON

1. I have a British accent.
2. I believe in experiencing art.
3. I am female.
4. P.L. Travers wrote a series of books about me.
5. Jane and Michael are my charges.
6. I am fictional.
7. I am known to pop in and pop out.
8. My film won five Academy Awards® in 1964, including Best Actress and Best Song.
9. I worked for the Banks, but I know nothing of investments.
10. My carpetbag is much bigger than it looks.
11. I worked at Number 17 Cherry Tree Lane.
12. I tend to leave when the wind changes.
13. I enjoy flying kites.
14. Walt Disney made a movie about me.
15. I advocate taking medication with sugar.
16. Some have called me "Nanny."
17. I have a good friend who is a chimney sweep.
18. I always travel with an umbrella.
19. Julie Andrews played me in a movie.
20. Supercalifragilisticexpialidocious!

6

PEOPLE

I AM MARY POPPINS

I AM A PERSON

1. I am a US civil rights leader.
2. I was born in Atlanta, Georgia.
3. I am an African American.
4. I am male.
5. I am the King of nonviolent protest.
6. I fought against racism.
7. I am an author.
8. I was arrested and jailed.
9. I won the Nobel Peace Prize.
10. I wrote the famous "Letter from Birmingham Jail."
11. My holiday occurs every January.
12. I am a doctor but I do not practice medicine.
13. I was assassinated by James Earl Ray.
14. I am no longer living.
15. My wife's name is Coretta Scott.
16. I led a march on Washington.
17. I have a dream.
18. Jesse Jackson followed me.
19. I am named after a reformation leader.
20. I am a pastor.

7

PEOPLE

I AM MARTIN LUTHER KING, JR.

I AM A PERSON

1. You may have read about me.
2. I hate Who-hash.
3. My heart was two sizes too small.
4. My only companion is a dog.
5. I live on a tall mountain.
6. I don't like Christmas.
7. I live near Who-ville.
8. Dr. Seuss created me.
9. I'm green.
10. I'm a mean one.
11. I tried to steal a holiday.
12. I don't like noise.
13. I pretended to be Santa Claus.
14. You might watch me on TV every year.
15. My soul is filled with spiders.
16. I know Cindy Lou Who, do you?
17. I, myself, carved the roast beast.
18. I am male.
19. Jim Carrey plays me in a movie.
20. I am fictional.

8

PEOPLE

I AM THE GRINCH

I AM A PERSON

1. I live under the name of Sanders.
2. My Robin doesn't have a red breast.
3. I am British.
4. There's a house at my corner.
5. I'm known for being stout, not smart.
6. I've been scared of my own tracks.
7. I love to eat, but I'm always stuffed.
8. I show up in stories that a father told to his son.
9. It all started *When We Were Very Young*.
10. My real name is Edward Bear.
11. My story was first published in 1926.
12. I'm not scary but my last name rhymes with "boo."
13. I live in the Hundred Acre Woods.
14. My friends include a donkey, a rabbit, a tiger and a boy.
15. My last name makes children giggle.
16. My middle name is "the."
17. I've braved bees and trees for honey.
18. I am animated by Disney.
19. Ernest H. Shepard drew me.
20. I hope that people will bear with me.

9

PEOPLE

I AM WINNIE-THE-POOH

I AM A PERSON

1. My favorite color is green.
2. Disney made a movie about me.
3. I taught my shadow tricks.
4. I can fly, but I'm not a bird.
5. James Barrie created me.
6. I know the Darling family.
7. I fight crocodiles and pirates.
8. I once lost my shadow.
9. Tiger Lily is a friend of mine.
10. My favorite fairy is Tinkerbell.
11. I am make-believe.
12. Captain Hook is my enemy.
13. I never wanted to grow up.
14. I live in Neverland.
15. My gang is a bunch of Lost Boys.
16. I share my first name with a famous rabbit.
17. My friends and I are orphans.
18. My initials are P.P.
19. I love to have fun.
20. Robin Williams played me in the movies.

10

PEOPLE

I AM PETER PAN

I AM A PERSON

1. I am the first US President.
2. I am the "father of our country."
3. You learn about me in school.
4. I am no longer living.
5. I am from Virginia.
6. I am an American.
7. People carry my picture in their wallets.
8. People celebrate my birthday.
9. My ideas are revolutionary.
10. I said I chopped down a cherry tree.
11. My wife's name is Martha.
12. I might have said, "Father, I cannot tell a lie."
13. I am a general.
14. A state and a city are named after me.
15. John Adams was my V.P.
16. I wear a white wig.
17. Mt. Vernon is my home.
18. A monument to me stands in Washington, D.C.
19. I fought in the French and Indian War.
20. My face is carved into Mount Rushmore.

11

PEOPLE

I AM GEORGE WASHINGTON

I AM A PERSON

1. I speak Spanish.
2. I carry a Map and a Backpack.
3. I am female.
4. Sometimes I like to visit my Abuela's house.
5. I have a Mami and a Papi.
6. I have my own TV show on Nick Jr.
7. I have a friend named Boots.
8. I like to search for clues.
9. I am an adventurer and a problem solver.
10. I like to find new places.
11. You can buy my videos and DVDs.
12. I know that ice cream in Spanish is *el helado*.
13. I have a friend named Tico.
14. I am seven years old.
15. I am Latina.
16. I know a fox named Swiper.
17. I am totally animated.
18. I have brown hair and brown eyes.
19. I've visited The Spooky Forest and Crocodile Lake.
20. I made friends with a Little Star.

12

PEOPLE

I AM DORA THE EXPLORER

I AM A PERSON

1. I am the subject of a novel.
2. I am the subject of many movies.
3. I have quite an overbite.
4. I am eastern European.
5. I'm a Count but you won't see me on *Sesame Street*.
6. I'm a real sucker.
7. I live in a castle.
8. I am centuries old.
9. I come to life at night.
10. I like real bloody Marys.
11. I was staked out in the end.
12. I am male.
13. You'll never smell garlic on my breath.
14. I can be found hanging around.
15. I'm a real die-hard.
16. I scare people.
17. My eating habits are horrifying.
18. Days can be deadly for me.
19. I prefer a liquid diet.
20. I wore black long before it was fashionable.

13

PEOPLE

I AM DRACULA

I AM A PERSON

1. I have a beautiful singing voice.
2. I am an excellent swimmer.
3. Disney brought me to the movies.
4. I traded my voice to the Sea Witch for legs.
5. I am an animated character.
6. My father is a king.
7. I am 16 years old.
8. Sebastian is my crabby friend.
9. Hans Christian Anderson wrote my story.
10. I used to be part girl, part fish.
11. I lived under the sea.
12. I have beautiful red hair.
13. One of my friends is a flounder.
14. I am curious about humans.
15. My father is a merman.
16. I am fictional.
17. I fell in love with Prince Eric.
18. I comb my hair with a Dinglehopper.
19. I am female.
20. I had three days to get a prince to kiss me.

14

PEOPLE

I AM ARIEL, THE LITTLE MERMAID

I AM A PERSON

1. I am not real.
2. I am a boy.
3. J.K. Rowling tells my stories.
4. I know a prisoner from Azkaban.
5. I'm from England.
6. My story will be told in seven books.
7. I wear glasses.
8. I use brooms, but not for sweeping.
9. I go to a school for wizards.
10. Daniel Radcliffe played me in the movies.
11. I won my school tournament the first time I played.
12. I am a young wizard in training.
13. If you know Diagon Alley, then you know me.
14. My favorite pastime is playing Quidditch.
15. Hogwarts is my school.
16. I have a distinctive scar on my forehead.
17. Owls deliver my mail.
18. I have a friend named Hermione.
19. I am an orphan.
20. My cousin is named Dudley Dursley.

15

PEOPLE

I AM HARRY POTTER

I AM A PERSON

1. For five years I played Moesha on TV.
2. My last name is Norwood.
3. Once, I sang about "Sittin' Up in My Room."
4. I have a brother named Ray J.
5. I am a Cover Girl.
6. I am female.
7. "I Wanna Be Down."
8. My TV show was cancelled in 2001.
9. I am an American.
10. I sang "What About Us?"
11. I share my name with a kind of liquor.
12. Like Cher and Madonna, I use only one name.
13. I was born in 1979.
14. I am one of the VH1 divas.
15. I was in *I Still Know What You Did Last Summer.*
16. I went to the prom with Kobe Bryant.
17. I am from Mississippi.
18. I played Cinderella in a TV movie.
19. I went *Double Platinum* with Diana Ross.
20. I am a pop singer and an actress.

16

PEOPLE

I AM BRANDY

I AM A PERSON

1. I was born in Kansas.
2. I was lost somewhere between New Guinea and Howland Island.
3. I am female.
4. I disappeared with Frederic J. Noonan in 1937.
5. I am American.
6. No one knows where I ended up.
7. I learned to fly in California.
8. I was the first woman to fly over the Atlantic as a passenger.
9. I attended Columbia University.
10. My disappearance is a mystery.
11. I loved to fly but I did not have wings.
12. I once worked as a nurse.
13. I saw my first airplane when I was 10 years old.
14. I first flew over the Atlantic in 1928.
15. I tried to fly around the world.
16. Some say I may have been taken captive by the Japanese.
17. I was born in 1898.
18. I married George Palmer Putnam.
19. I am a pilot.
20. I was an early female aviator.

17

PEOPLE

I AM AMELIA EARHART

I AM A PERSON

1. San Francisco is my kind of town.
2. I set the home run record in 2001.
3. I was a Pirate before I grew up to be a Giant.
4. I wear number 25.
5. I am a professional athlete.
6. I am the king of splash landings.
7. My father was a baseball player, just like me.
8. I like to steal, but I'm not a criminal.
9. I'm a living American.
10. I wear black and orange to work.
11. My cousin is Reggie Jackson.
12. Candlestick was my backyard.
13. I hit 73 home runs in one season.
14. My initials are B.B.
15. In 2001, I was MVP for the fourth time.
16. I beat the Babe, Sammy and Mark.
17. I wear one earring.
18. I have a strong swing.
19. I am male.
20. My bats don't hang out in caves.

18

PEOPLE

I AM BARRY BONDS

I AM A PERSON

1. I am an athlete.
2. My dad trained me to be the best.
3. I am the youngest golfer to win a career Grand Slam.
4. My name is Eldrick, but no one calls me that.
5. I live in Florida.
6. I left Stanford to go pro in 1996.
7. I'm a wild cat on the golf course.
8. You can see me on a box of Wheaties.
9. I like to putter around.
10. I've mastered my game.
11. My last name is a word for forest.
12. My foundation helps kids play golf.
13. I've been Sports Illustrated's Sportsman of the Year.
14. I was born in the 1970s.
15. My favorite movie is *Caddyshack*.
16. I played golf on TV at two years old.
17. My peers voted me "PGA Tour Player of the Year."
18. I have done some work for Nike™.
19. My heritage is African American and Asian.
20. In 1999, I earned a record $6.5 million.

19

PEOPLE

I AM TIGER WOODS

I AM A PERSON

1. I am a fictional male.
2. I have a secret identity.
3. When I was little, my parents were murdered.
4. Terry McGinnis goes Beyond me.
5. Commissioner Gordon knows me but he doesn't know who I really am.
6. During the 1960s I had my own TV show.
7. I am a very wealthy bachelor.
8. I wish decks of cards didn't come with jokers.
9. Val Kilmer, George Clooney and Michael Keaton all know me.
10. I take the law into my own hands.
11. I've dated Vicki Vale.
12. My favorite animal is a nocturnal mammal that sleeps upside down.
13. I have a butler named Alfred Pennyworth.
14. I wear a cape but I'm not Superman.
15. Sometimes I act kind of batty.
16. I live in Wayne Manor.
17. Dick Grayson and I fight criminals together.
18. My first name is Bruce.
19. My Robin doesn't build nests.
20. I've had many enemies, including Penguin, Two-Face and The Riddler.

20
PEOPLE

I AM BATMAN

I AM A PERSON

1. I know a guy named Justin pretty well.
2. I am a pop star.
3. I have done some ads for Pepsi.
4. My name only has one "T" in it.
5. I am female.
6. My first record was … *Baby One More Time*.
7. I am from Louisiana.
8. I brought a snake to the MTV Video Awards.
9. My third album is named after me.
10. You can usually see my belly button.
11. I was a member of the Mickey Mouse Club.
12. I have blonde hair.
13. I married–and divorced–in January 2004.
14. In 2000, *Oops! … I Did It Again*.
15. I made a movie called *Crossroads*.
16. I am a cover girl.
17. My last name sounds like a hunting tool.
18. I worship Madonna, but she's no saint.
19. My initials are B.S.
20. I work for Jive Records.

21

PEOPLE

I AM BRITNEY SPEARS

I AM A PERSON

1. I was born in Philadelphia.
2. George Washington was a friend of mine.
3. They say I put stars and stripes on the flag.
4. I was born in 1752.
5. I made flags during a revolution.
6. I am a famous seamstress.
7. No one knows if my story is true.
8. I am American.
9. My parents were Quakers.
10. I was born Elizabeth Griscom.
11. My grandson, William J. Caney, made my story famous.
12. My favorite colors are red, white and blue.
13. I married three times.
14. I died in 1836.
15. You learn about me in history.
16. I made my living from an upholstery business.
17. I completed my first flag right before the Declaration of Independence.
18. My flag had 13 stars in a circle.
19. I lived to be 84.
20. My famous work has 13 stripes.

22

PEOPLE

I AM BETSY ROSS

I AM A PERSON

1. Vrroom … my initials are V.W.
2. I live in Florida.
3. I am an athlete.
4. My last name is one of the most popular in the US.
5. I have won at Wimbledon.
6. A Roman goddess and I have the same name.
7. Sometimes I compete against my sister.
8. I am female and over 6'1" tall.
9. My father is my coach and manager.
10. I was born in 1980.
11. In my racket, sneakers are worn.
12. I share my name with a planet.
13. I design my own clothes for work.
14. Serena is my younger sister.
15. I won Olympic gold.
16. When I'm at work, I'm not looking for love.
17. I went pro at 14.
18. I was *Sports Illustrated's* Sportswoman of the Year in 2000.
19. When I started out, I wore beads.
20. I share my last name with a funny Robin.

23

PEOPLE

I AM VENUS WILLIAMS

I AM A PERSON

1. I am a living female.
2. I was born in Houston, TX on September 28, 1987.
3. I am an actress and a singer.
4. *Santa Claus Lane* is the name of my Christmas album.
5. You can catch me on TV and at the movies.
6. I've worked for Disney but I've never been on *The Mickey Mouse Club*.
7. I performed as a ballerina when I was six.
8. I had a #1 single but it's like, "So Yesterday."
9. I performed at the American Music Awards in 2003.
10. I co-starred in the movie *Agent Cody Banks*.
11. My band members' nicknames are Rone-Shoelaces, Fiver, Baby, Walker and Double-Shot.
12. Britney Spears is a fan of mine.
13. Ashton Kutcher and I were both in the movie *Cheaper by the Dozen*.
14. My older sister Haylie is also a musician.
15. In 2003, I released my album *Metamorphosis*.
16. Due to my popularity, I've been called a "Tween Queen."
17. You've probably seen my character, Lizzie McGuire, on TV and at the movies.
18. My initials are H.D.
19. You can catch my TV show on ABC on Saturday mornings.
20. My friends call me Hil.

24

PEOPLE

I AM HILARY DUFF

PLACES

I AM A PLACE

1. Six nations have flown their flags over me.
2. I am in America.
3. I was the 28th to join my union.
4. I like Ike. He's one of my native sons.
5. I have a panhandle.
6. My toast has nothing to do with drinking.
7. I house NASA's Johnson Space Center.
8. My largest city is named for Sam.
9. I border Mexico.
10. Most people prefer red, but my favorite rose is yellow.
11. I was biggest until Alaska.
12. Although I only have one star, I'm not really alone.
13. I'm a five-letter state.
14. Don't mess with me.
15. My baseball team is named for law enforcement officers.
16. Everything is bigger in me.
17. People sing about being deep in my heart.
18. I still remember the Alamo.
19. I'm not greasy, but I boast a quarter of the U.S.'s oil.
20. George W. Bush calls me home.

1

PLACES

I AM TEXAS

I AM A PLACE

1. When people visit me, I take their breath away.
2. Jon Krakauer wrote about me.
3. Yes sir, I was named for a George.
4. I always feel like I'm on top of the world.
5. I was formed about 60 millions years ago.
6. I'm always feeling high.
7. I'm always cold.
8. Come see me if someone tells you to take a hike.
9. Avalanches have caused most of my fatalities.
10. I'm covered in snow.
11. I'm on the border of Tibet.
12. Sir Edmund Hilary is best known for climbing all over me.
13. I'm located in the Himalayas.
14. In 1999, I was found to be six feet higher than previously thought.
15. The Khumbu Ice Fall is my most dangerous area.
16. I'm not a cemetery, but there are approximately 120 corpses on my grounds.
17. Sherpas know me best.
18. In Nepal, I'm called "The Goddess of the Sky."
19. I'm the highest of my kind in the world.
20. My English name identifies the first person that recorded my height and location.

2

PLACES

I AM MT. EVEREST

I AM A PLACE

1. I am tropical.
2. I'm an island.
3. Christopher Columbus discovered me in 1492.
4. I am definitely not American.
5. Spanish is my official language.
6. I have a bay named after hoofed animals that roll in the mud.
7. I am the largest island in the West Indies.
8. Baseball has been very good to me.
9. I was once home to Hemmingway.
10. I live on sugar.
11. The Buena Vista Social Club brought my music to the big screen.
12. I taught Ricky Ricardo how to play the drums.
13. In the 1970s and 1980s I assisted Soviet-supported movements.
14. I am known for cigars.
15. Many of my people reside in Florida.
16. I had a missile crisis during JFK's days.
17. If you're a US citizen, you probably haven't visited me.
18. The Pope came to visit me in 1998.
19. The US has a long-standing embargo against me.
20. I won a famous custody battle in 2000.

3

PLACES

I AM CUBA

I AM A PLACE

1. I was born in 1971.
2. I am home to Liberty Square.
3. I am twice the size of New York City.
4. I have a castle, but I am not ruled by a king.
5. You will see lots of animals if you visit me.
6. I am in the US.
7. I'm located on 43 square miles of former swampland.
8. I am one of the happiest places on earth.
9. I saw 10 million people in 1971.
10. My creator never saw me.
11. I am in the Sunshine State.
12. Every night I light up the sky.
13. You may go head over heels when you visit me.
14. I've got mice that aren't afraid of cats.
15. You can see Pluto when you visit me.
16. My entire town shuts down and is thoroughly cleaned every single night.
17. Las Vegas is the only place with more hotels than me.
18. I love to be visited by kids of all ages.
19. I am one of the most visited tourist attractions in the world.
20. I've got land in California.

4

PLACES

I AM WALT DISNEY WORLD

I AM A PLACE

1. I have lots of cows and few people.
2. People visit me for hiking and fishing.
3. November 8, 1889 is a big date for me.
4. My flower is bitterroot.
5. I am the 41st US state.
6. I have seen lots of cowboys and Indians.
7. I had my share of gold rushes.
8. I saw Custer's Last Stand.
9. My capital is named after a woman.
10. I have the third lowest population density in the US.
11. I see the Continental Divide.
12. Jimmy Buffet sings about my Livingston.
13. Writer Thomas McGuane lives in me.
14. I have lots of dude ranches.
15. I border Canada.
16. I'm home to Glacier National Park.
17. The Dakotas border me.
18. Don't confuse me with a famous quarterback.
19. My name means "mountain" in Spanish.
20. My nickname is Big Sky Country.

5

PLACES

I AM MONTANA

I AM A PLACE

1. My climate is semi-tropical.
2. I have thousands of miles of waterways.
3. I'm American.
4. I became a state in 1812.
5. I am named for a king.
6. Rice is a major crop for me.
7. I was the 18th state to join the US.
8. The Choctaw Indians were among my first inhabitants.
9. My Saints never met Roger Moore.
10. I am located in the South.
11. My nickname is The Pelican State.
12. Translated, my capital's name is "Red Stick."
13. I am the US leader in shrimp production.
14. I border Texas.
15. The Mississippi River flows through me.
16. I was bought from the French in 1803.
17. I am shaped like a boot.
18. Huey Long is my Kingfish.
19. Many of my cooks are Cajun.
20. My largest city is home to the Sugar Bowl.

6

PLACES

I AM LOUISIANA

I AM A PLACE

1. My climate is temperate.
2. I am a city.
3. You can find palm trees on my boulevards.
4. I am in North America.
5. My altitude is 7,350 feet.
6. I am located at the foot of two magnificent snow-covered volcanoes.
7. In 1551, the first university in North America was founded in me.
8. I hosted the Olympics in 1968.
9. My latitude is about the same as Bombay, India.
10. I have a population of over 25 million.
11. My subway system is called the Metro.
12. Cortez discovered me in 1519.
13. The Pyramid of the Sun is nearby.
14. My markets feature Indian arts and handicrafts.
15. The name of my country is in my name.
16. I was once the site of the capital city of the Aztec Empire.
17. Most of my inhabitants speak Spanish.
18. Montezuma's palace was located here.
19. Diego Rivera decorated my buildings.
20. I have a serious air pollution problem.

7

PLACES

I AM MEXICO CITY, MEXICO

I AM A PLACE

1. I was important in 1864.
2. I was Marthasville and Terminus before I was me.
3. I am the largest city in my state.
4. My people eat at the Waffle House after midnight.
5. I'm 600 miles southwest of Washington, D.C.
6. I am the seat of Fulton County.
7. I have over twenty colleges and universities.
8. I am the capital of the Empire State of the South.
9. I'm six miles southeast of the Chattahoochee River.
10. Coca-Cola calls me home.
11. I'm near Stone Mountain and Six Flags.
12. I am home to Dr. Martin Luther King's Ebenezer Baptist Church.
13. *Gone With the Wind* author Margaret Mitchell hails from me.
14. Ted Turner has been a local resident of mine.
15. My Flames burn on ice.
16. My Braves aren't Indians.
17. I'm home to Hawks and Falcons.
18. My state is known for peaches and bulldogs.
19. I hosted the 1996 Summer Olympics.
20. My Georgia was never in the USSR.

8

PLACES

I AM ATLANTA, GEORGIA

I AM A PLACE

1. I was divided in 1920.
2. I am an island.
3. My people have been persecuted.
4. I am European.
5. Most of my people are Roman Catholic.
6. I am home to the Cliffs of Moher.
7. Green and orange are my colors.
8. Cead Mile Failte is a motto of mine.
9. My beers can be stout.
10. My green is legendary.
11. I contain the Lakes of Killarney.
12. George Bernard Shaw is one of my natives.
13. My inhabitants make Waterford Crystal.
14. According to legend, St. Patrick drove out all my snakes.
15. Some people call me Erin.
16. My eyes have been known to smile.
17. I suffered the Great Potato Famine.
18. My people are the mascot of Notre Dame University.
19. I am associated with leprechauns.
20. Kiss my Blarney Stone and you'll never be the same.

9

PLACES

I AM IRELAND

I AM A PLACE

1. Red is my favorite color.
2. Your class won't be taking a field trip to visit me.
3. I'm fourth in a well-known line-up.
4. Someone sent Rover right over to me.
5. Phobos and Deimos are always hanging around me.
6. My climate is almost always cold.
7. I am big and round.
8. I have craters but I'm not the Moon.
9. Recent pictures of me have caused quite a stir.
10. I am part of the Solar System.
11. Nissan didn't make my Pathfinder.
12. Though I'm considered close by, you've never visited me.
13. I am a planet.
14. Some people think creepy-looking aliens live on me.
15. I sometimes appear in science fiction stories.
16. I was named after the Roman god of war.
17. Scramble the letters of my name and you've got arms.
18. I'm not Jupiter or Venus.
19. Kids say they'd come to me to eat candy bars.
20. Scientists talk about colonizing me.

10

PLACES

I AM MARS

I AM A PLACE

1. In the 1500s, Hernando De Soto explored me.
2. I am American.
3. In 1796, I became the 16th US state.
4. I was the last state to secede from the Union and the first to be readmitted.
5. Come to me and see Rock City.
6. Georgia and Missouri both border me.
7. I was once part of North Carolina.
8. My largest city sees Federal Express every night.
9. You can see seven states from me.
10. Davy Crockett served me in Congress.
11. Martin Luther King, Jr. was assassinated in me.
12. You'll find the Great Smoky Mountains within me.
13. Andrew Jackson called me home.
14. I share my name with a famous American playwright.
15. I have three sets of double letters.
16. I'm known for my volunteers.
17. Kentucky is one of my neighbors.
18. The Grateful Dead say, "There ain't no place I'd rather be" than mine.
19. I am home to Graceland.
20. My capital is the home of country music.

11

PLACES

I AM TENNESSEE

I AM A PLACE

1. I have been on my own since 1961.
2. I am a country.
3. I was part of the Commonwealth.
4. I am in the Southern Hemisphere.
5. I have the most highly industrialized economy on my continent.
6. Cricket is one of my national pastimes.
7. I'm home to the Kalahari Desert.
8. I am African.
9. I know some real Boers.
10. I am a producer of diamonds.
11. English is my national language.
12. I am a major world producer of gold.
13. Namibia, Botswana and Zimbabwe are my neighbors.
14. Lesotho lies inside me.
15. If you were marching to Pretoria, you'd be marching toward me.
16. I touch two oceans.
17. I contain Good Hope.
18. For me, everything was black and white.
19. My largest city is named after Johan.
20. My apartheid policies were well known.

12

PLACES

I AM SOUTH AFRICA

I AM A PLACE

1. I am located north of the equator.
2. I am American.
3. I am home to many stars, but no planets.
4. You may see me in the movies.
5. I am found in California.
6. Sunset and Vine are my streets.
7. I am a city.
8. I've got famous Hills.
9. My name suggests that I am a type of timber.
10. My fame started in the Twentieth Century.
11. My name is on a hill.
12. I can see the Pacific Ocean.
13. Many visit me to catch a rising star.
14. I am the world's movie capital.
15. My name lights up at night.
16. A lot of movie stars live in me.
17. There are lots of songs about me.
18. I live near Disneyland.
19. My Chinese Theatre is a popular place to visit.
20. I have a sidewalk with stars on it.

13

PLACES

I AM HOLLYWOOD

I AM A PLACE

1. I am a national park.
2. I get my name from high yellow cliffs you can see in me.
3. I'm one of the first of my kind.
4. I have geysers and hot springs.
5. I'm great for hiking and camping.
6. Over two million people visit me yearly.
7. Part of me is in Wyoming.
8. I am America's largest wildlife preserve.
9. I have bears, elk and bison.
10. I am covered with snow all winter.
11. I am partly in Montana.
12. You can visit Fort Yellowstone in me.
13. I came with the Louisiana Purchase.
14. Eagle Peak is my highest point.
15. I have waterfalls and forests.
16. Come to me to see Old Faithful.
17. I have 1000 miles of trails.
18. 80% of me is forest.
19. I have a Grand Canyon.
20. Theodore Roosevelt helped protect me.

14

PLACES

I AM YELLOWSTONE NATIONAL PARK

I AM A PLACE

1. I have a Golden Gate.
2. Visit me and ride a cable car.
3. I had a serious earthquake in 1989.
4. I am a city.
5. I am home to the 49ers.
6. I have Alcatraz and Treasure Islands.
7. I am on the West Coast.
8. I am in California.
9. I am on a peninsula.
10. I have Fisherman's Wharf, Telegraph Hill and Chinatown.
11. I am in America.
12. I grew a lot during the gold rush.
13. I have a famous pyramid.
14. My name has two words.
15. My dough is sour.
16. The United Nations charter was drafted here.
17. I have steep hills.
18. Sea lions like my Fisherman's Wharf.
19. Many have left their hearts in me.
20. I am a treat to visit.

15

PLACES

I AM SAN FRANCISCO, CALIFORNIA

I AM A PLACE

1. I'm hard to see when I'm new.
2. I am not made of green cheese.
3. It's easy to see me at night.
4. I orbit around the earth.
5. I fly an American flag.
6. Humans first visited me by spaceship in 1969.
7. I am smaller than the Earth.
8. You can see me from anywhere.
9. Neil Armstrong was the first person to visit me.
10. People talk about the man in me.
11. One side of me is always dark.
12. Wolves like to howl at me.
13. Some are superstitious about me when I am full.
14. I am miles from the Earth.
15. I am as old as the Earth.
16. A cow jumped over me in a nursery rhyme.
17. I reflect light from the sun.
18. I'm yellow in Lucky Charms® cereal.
19. My pull affects the ocean's tides.
20. I can go from quarter to half to full without changing size.

I AM THE MOON

I AM A PLACE

1. I am a country.
2. My queen was nicknamed "Bloody Mary."
3. My money is measured in pounds.
4. My people speak with English accents.
5. I am in Europe.
6. I am Shakespeare's homeland.
7. Cricket is my national sport.
8. London is my capital.
9. Tweed helps keep us warm.
10. America was once my colony.
11. I am the largest country in the United Kingdom.
12. If you play my football, you can't use your hands.
13. My soldiers wore red coats.
14. The Channel connects me to France.
15. Sir Isaac Newton was born here.
16. My people call elevators "lifts."
17. Teatime is one of my traditions.
18. My Yorkshire pudding isn't dessert.
19. The North Sea is east of me.
20. I'm part of an island.

17

PLACES

I AM ENGLAND

I AM A PLACE

1. I am a state.
2. Hollywood is part of me.
3. I border the Pacific Ocean.
4. Visit Disneyland and you visit me.
5. There is a brown bear on my state flag.
6. I contain America's lowest point.
7. My redwoods are the tallest trees in the world.
8. My condor is the largest bird in North America.
9. I am known as "The Golden State."
10. Los Angeles is my biggest city.
11. I am bordered by Oregon, Nevada, Arizona and Mexico.
12. My best shopping is on Rodeo Drive.
13. I am home to part of Lake Tahoe.
14. I have beaches and ski resorts.
15. The Sierras are my mountains.
16. My capital is Sacramento.
17. I saw a gold rush in 1848.
18. You can find Angels here.
19. I have earthquakes and floods.
20. My wineries are some of the best in the world.

18

PLACES

I AM CALIFORNIA

I AM A PLACE

1. John Wesley Powell gave this site its name.
2. You'll find a river at the bottom of me.
3. The Colorado River made me.
4. I am in America.
5. Copper was found in my rocks.
6. I am in Arizona.
7. I am called "The Spectacular Valley."
8. I am known for my natural beauty.
9. I am out of doors.
10. I expose layers of rock.
11. I see three million visitors annually.
12. Some people ride mules in me.
13. I am considered one of earth's great natural wonders.
14. I began six million years ago.
15. I'm a deep valley with steep sides.
16. My rocks are two billion years old.
17. A river eroded layers of rock to form me.
18. I am a favorite hiking area.
19. I became a national park in 1919.
20. *The Brady Bunch* vacationed here.

19

PLACES

I AM THE GRAND CANYON

I AM A PLACE

1. I am the southernmost state in the US.
2. My people hula without hoops.
3. My natives are called "Polynesians."
4. My alphabet has only 12 letters.
5. Visit me and you might attend a luau.
6. I was originally called the Sandwich Islands.
7. I am not in the continental US.
8. I have black beaches.
9. I am a favorite vacation spot.
10. I am the 50th state.
11. Honolulu is my capital.
12. Magnum P.I. once called me home.
13. My people tell stories with their hands.
14. My agriculture includes coffee and macadamia nuts.
15. I might greet you with an aloha.
16. I contain 132 islands, reefs and shoals.
17. I was formed by volcanoes.
18. I am famous for my warm weather.
19. I am in the Pacific Ocean.
20. Pearl Harbor is located here.

20

PLACES

I AM HAWAII

I AM A PLACE

1. I am in America.
2. I am named for a US president.
3. Maryland and Virginia donated land to me.
4. I am a Capital City.
5. I am home to Capital Hill.
6. My Redskins don't live in teepees.
7. I've housed former US leaders.
8. Concerts are played at my monument named after a former president.
9. The Potomac River flows by me.
10. My initials stand for District of Columbia.
11. I can see the Lincoln Memorial.
12. I house America's largest library.
13. You can see me on TV.
14. The Smithsonian Institution is here.
15. I am a tourist attraction.
16. Every year I host the Cherry Blossom Festival.
17. The Supreme Court meets in me.
18. Visit me and visit the White House.
19. Congress makes my laws.
20. My famous zoo has pandas.

21

PLACES

I AM WASHINGTON D.C.

I AM A PLACE

1. I am a city.
2. I was once my country's capital.
3. I am home to the United Nations.
4. I am American.
5. My garden on Madison Square is no bed of roses.
6. My old name was New Amsterdam.
7. If you've been on Broadway, you've been to me.
8. I have the Brooklyn Bridge.
9. My Yankees never fought in the Civil War.
10. The subway is my favorite transportation.
11. The Statue of Liberty can see me.
12. Immigrants came to my Ellis Island.
13. I have Queens, but no kings.
14. Central Park is found in me.
15. I house the Empire State Building.
16. Many of my streets are numbered.
17. My jets fly in New Jersey.
18. My cabs are yellow.
19. I have Grand Central Station.
20. They call me the Big Apple.

22

PLACES

I AM NEW YORK CITY

I AM A PLACE

1. I speak several languages.
2. The Ural Mountains form my eastern border.
3. I contain Greece and Norway.
4. Americans cross the sea to see me.
5. The Holy Roman Empire was here.
6. I'm the second smallest of my kind.
7. I make really fast luxury cars.
8. The Mediterranean Sea separates me from Africa.
9. I am a continent.
10. I am not in the United States.
11. I cover 7% of the world's area.
12. To Americans, I'm foreign.
13. The Arctic Ocean is to my north.
14. I am the second largest continent in population.
15. My borders are changing.
16. I have more than 20 countries.
17. I'm the opposite of "I'm down."
18. I've inspired painters, writers and singers.
19. France and Germany are part of me.
20. I have an East and a West.

23

PLACES

I AM EUROPE

I AM A PLACE

1. I resemble a marble.
2. I am a planet.
3. I am the closest planet to Mars.
4. Geologists study my make-up.
5. I am the fifth largest planet.
6. Rearrange my letters and they spell "heart."
7. I have a crust, but I'm not a pie.
8. I'm always moving.
9. My inside is made of hot rocks.
10. People used to think that I was flat.
11. Every time I spin around, a day passes.
12. I am afraid of losing my ozone layers.
13. Dinosaurs used to live on me.
14. I travel around the Sun.
15. About 70% of me is water.
16. I have one moon.
17. How I was created has been the talk of ages.
18. I am at least 4.5 billion years old.
19. I weigh 6000 billion tons.
20. I have seven continents.

24

PLACES

I AM EARTH

I AM A THING

1. A lot of people fall for me.
2. I like winters better than summers.
3. I'll cost you quite a few greenbacks.
4. I'm not a biker, but I appreciate a good helmet.
5. I'm mostly flat, but I do have a nice curve or two.
6. My popularity surged in the 1990s.
7. Ross Rebagliati won the gold medal at my Olympic premiere in 1998.
8. I am more popular with youngsters than oldsters.
9. I am required equipment in some sport events.
10. You'll find me in the X-Games.
11. I am a mode of transportation.
12. I love speed.
13. My binding has nothing to do with book publishing.
14. I get off on bumps, jumps and humps.
15. I get really psyched when I see a mountain.
16. Some of my biggest advocates go surfing in the summer.
17. People stand on me when I'm doing my thing.
18. I'm not a smoker, but I get excited when I see a half pipe.
19. I am more than two feet long and less than seven feet long.
20. I am typically found in ski resorts, but I'm not skis.

1

THINGS

I AM A SNOWBOARD

I AM A THING

1. I am Asian.
2. I am popular with beginning pianists.
3. Some people find me hard to handle.
4. You won't find me in Thailand.
5. I got my start in the Shang Dynasty around 1766 B.C.
6. Sometimes I come with instructions.
7. I have a tapered physique.
8. Some people catch flies with me.
9. I am long and thin.
10. Like shoes, I come by the pair.
11. Sometimes women stick me in their hair.
12. Mulan used me in the Disney animated film.
13. I don't go with pizza or burgers.
14. I like eating.
15. My use requires fine motor skills.
16. I am usually made of wood or plastic.
17. Some people use me as drumsticks.
18. I'm a utensil.
19. I need you to lend me a hand.
20. People expect to see me in Chinese restaurants.

2

THINGS

I AM CHOPSTICKS

I AM A THING

1. Rock stars and celebrities drop by to work with me on a weekly basis.
2. My grandma is named Jacqueline Bouvier.
3. My family has five members.
4. My favorite animal is a fox.
5. My family shops at the Quickie Mart.
6. My aunts work at the DMV.
7. Sam Simon helps write my story.
8. Tracy Ullman gave me my start.
9. The head of my household works for a nuclear power plant.
10. My youngest member doesn't talk.
11. Jebediah Springfield founded my town.
12. Julie Kavner speaks for one of me.
13. Mr. Burns and Smithers like to boss one of me around.
14. I am a prime time TV series.
15. Santa's Little Helper is my family's best friend.
16. I know a Krusty clown.
17. Matt Groening created me.
18. I've made an appearance at the Festival of Animation.
19. I am not related to O.J. Simpson.
20. I have something in common with *The Flintstones*.

3

THINGS

I AM *THE SIMPSONS*

I AM A THING

1. I can come in colors but I'm usually white.
2. I never move but I have moveable parts.
3. You've seen many of my kind.
4. I never leave my room.
5. You had no use for me when you were a baby.
6. I'm filled with water but I'm not an aquarium.
7. Sometimes I make a loud noise.
8. I'm made out of porcelain but I'm not fragile.
9. A special kind of paper is made just for me.
10. "Put a lid on it" is sometimes said about me.
11. I live in your house.
12. Using me is considered private.
13. People sit on me every day.
14. I have a special room all to myself.
15. Flushing, NY is my favorite city.
16. My bowl has nothing to do with football games.
17. My relatives are called bidets.
18. Guys know that I sometimes hang on the wall.
19. Plumbers know me.
20. In England, I hang out in the loo.

4

THINGS

I AM A TOILET

I AM A THING

1. I have a few enemies.
2. I resemble my southern relatives.
3. I blend in with my surroundings.
4. Few have seen me in my natural habitat.
5. I'm a good swimmer.
6. I rarely live past 15.
7. I can weigh up to a ton.
8. I am a mammal.
9. I am a favorite at the zoo.
10. I have a whale of an appetite.
11. If I took my coat off, you'd see that my skin is black.
12. I am carnivorous.
13. I'm not Rip Van Winkle, but I take long naps.
14. I own a fur coat.
15. I sleep in a den.
16. The colder, the better, as far as I am concerned.
17. I always wear white.
18. My cubs aren't scouts.
19. I symbolize the arctic.
20. You'll have to bear with me.

5

THINGS

I AM A POLAR BEAR

I AM A THING

1. My story was told by starting in the middle.
2. I am made up of six parts.
3. I happened a long, long time ago.
4. My Muppet isn't a *Sesame Street* regular.
5. My sabers are light.
6. You can see me at the movies.
7. I got my start in 1977.
8. I know twins named Leia and Luke.
9. I am told in two sets of trilogies.
10. Space travel is a breeze for me.
11. The force is with me, always.
12. As of 2004, my third episode is yet to be told.
13. Clones are an important part of my story.
14. I know Wookies, Ewoks and Space Slugs.
15. My planets include Naboo, Tatooine and Alderaan.
16. "I've got a bad feeling about this."
17. My Rebels fight the Empire.
18. I battled a Phantom Menace.
19. The Millennium Falcon has taken me far.
20. I know Obi-Wan Kenobi.

6

THINGS

I AM STAR WARS

I AM A THING

1. Sometimes I am quite alarming.
2. People like it when I am on time.
3. Sometimes I wear bells.
4. I have my own circular logic.
5. I'm a machine.
6. I've never been convicted of murder, but I've been accused of killing time.
7. I like to sit by your bed.
8. I get punched out at work.
9. My hours are numbered.
10. I have two hands but no legs.
11. I could be a grandfather, but not a grandson.
12. Wait a second — sometimes I have three hands.
13. I'm not a TV, but sometimes people watch me.
14. You can find me in a VCR, a car and a microwave oven.
15. I have a great memory when the lights go out.
16. I'm related to a sundial.
17. My face has no eyes and no expression.
18. I can be digital.
19. I like to hang on walls.
20. I get excited when I am all wound up.

7

THINGS

I AM A CLOCK

I AM A THING

1. I am an American institution.
2. I'm usually delivered.
3. I help raise money for a good cause.
4. I come in a box.
5. I only come around once a year.
6. I sometimes end up in the freezer.
7. I'm always associated with females.
8. I've seen a lot of milk in my time.
9. If you know Trefoil, you know me.
10. You can't find me in supermarkets.
11. My peanut butter doesn't come with jelly.
12. Despite me name, I'm made for boys too.
13. I'm a dieter's nightmare.
14. My girls wear green.
15. My lemons aren't sour.
16. My girls wear uniforms.
17. I can satisfy your sweet tooth.
18. I'm sold door-to-door.
19. When I'm thin, I'm minty.
20. My providers started as Guides; now they're Scouts.

8

THINGS

I AM GIRL SCOUT® COOKIES

I AM A THING

1. My Rome is not from Italy.
2. My jacks come in a cereal box.
3. I'm sweet.
4. A famous Johnny knows me well.
5. My history dates back to biblical times.
6. I'm no stranger to lunchboxes.
7. I spin on Beatles albums.
8. I can be red, green, pink or yellow.
9. My grannies aren't old.
10. My pie has nothing to do with 3.14159.
11. I've been known to keep doctors away.
12. I may show up in a pig's mouth.
13. If you like me, I could be "of your eye."
14. When I get smashed, I get sauced.
15. Unlike money, I grow on trees.
16. Sometimes people get confused and compare me to oranges.
17. My skin has a peel.
18. I helped Isaac Newton discover gravity.
19. When I'm Adam's, I have nothing to do with women.
20. I am a real fruit.

9

THINGS

I AM AN APPLE

I AM A THING

1. I am a Razor™ but I have no blade.
2. I'm back in vogue after decades of being ignored.
3. Sometimes I have a motor.
4. My wheels can be colorful.
5. My bunny hops aren't performed by rabbits.
6. I've been banned from schoolyards.
7. I can be folded up and put into a backpack.
8. I'm usually silver.
9. I brake a lot, but don't need to be fixed.
10. You'll love to handle my bars.
11. I'm powered by human feet.
12. I'm a mode of transportation.
13. I have wheels.
14. I can be a status symbol for kids.
15. Sometimes I have a light and shock absorbers.
16. I'm sold in toy stores.
17. I am a seven-letter word.
18. I'm not as fast as a car or bike.
19. My falls have nothing to do with water.
20. I'm usually found outdoors.

10

THINGS

I AM A SCOOTER

I AM A THING

1. I am big and ugly.
2. I am much older than you are.
3. I am carnivorous.
4. Part of my name means "king."
5. I appeared in *Toy Story*.
6. I always look green, whether I'm sick or not.
7. You might see me in a museum.
8. My bones are much bigger than yours.
9. Paleontologists know all about me.
10. Who are you calling a big mouth?
11. I had claws at the ends of my scrawny arms.
12. I stood about 12 feet tall.
13. I had about 50 huge teeth.
14. You may have seen me in *Jurassic Park*.
15. The last of my kind lived on Earth about 65 million years ago.
16. I know the Mesozoic Era better than the Paleozoic Era.
17. I am a dinosaur.
18. I had a pointy tail.
19. North America was my home.
20. I'm not a Triceratops or a Giganotosaurus.

11

THINGS

I AM TYRANNOSAURUS REX

I AM A THING

1. I need to get charged up every day to do my thing.
2. I've been called a public nuisance.
3. I have good hearing.
4. My ancestors often stayed by your bed or in the kitchen.
5. I can be a lifesaver in an emergency.
6. E.T. would have been much shorter if I had been around.
7. I've been known to distract drivers.
8. I might die on you.
9. Some speculate that I cause cancer.
10. Despite my name, I have nothing to do with molecular biology.
11. I can go almost anywhere you go.
12. Black is my favorite color.
13. I can play games with you.
14. I liked to be turned on.
15. I'm usually banned on airplanes.
16. I can reconnect you to your mother.
17. The word I hear most often is "hello."
18. I might not always give you a great reception.
19. I fit in your back pocket.
20. In England, I'm mobile.

12

THINGS

I AM A CELL PHONE

I AM A THING

1. I'm tall for my age.
2. I have stories that can't be told.
3. Superman can fly higher than me.
4. My flights are not on an airplane.
5. I have 3,194,547 light bulbs.
6. I took seven million man-hours to build.
7. I was completed in 1931.
8. Each year, I am struck by lightning more than 100 times.
9. I am closest to the N, R, B, D, F & Q.
10. I know Cary Grant and King Kong.
11. I have been the site of an annual vertical race since 1978.
12. I have 73 elevators.
13. In 1945, a plane crashed into me.
14. I play a pivotal role in *An Affair to Remember*.
15. I am located at 350 Fifth Avenue.
16. You can see me from New Jersey.
17. My initials are E.S.B.
18. I scrape the sky.
19. Tourists find me quite attractive.
20. I am in New York City.

13

THINGS

I AM THE EMPIRE STATE BUILDING

I AM A THING

1. I am an emergency vehicle.
2. I have a siren.
3. I am usually red or yellow.
4. I often have a ladder attached.
5. I carry several hoses.
6. Sometimes I help get cats out of trees.
7. I have wheels.
8. People make way when they hear me coming.
9. Little boys want to grow up to work with me.
10. I am an automobile.
11. My workers wear boots, coats and special helmets.
12. I carry an axe, a first-aid kit and a power saw.
13. I need fuel in order to work.
14. Sometimes I drive in parades.
15. I usually travel with an ambulance.
16. I'll come if you call 911.
17. Models of me are at toy stores.
18. I belong to the Fire Department.
19. When something is burning, I'm on my way.
20. I stay in an extra long garage.

14

THINGS

I AM A FIRE TRUCK

I AM A THING

1. I can be explosive.
2. I am part of the earth.
3. Mt. St. Helens is one of my kind.
4. I have a crater at my top.
5. I am active on the island of Hawaii.
6. I can throw piles of rock and dust into the air.
7. I create lava.
8. People like to keep their distance from me.
9. I can be hot.
10. My personality can be dormant, but I can be explosive from time to time.
11. I might blow my top.
12. Everything I touch turns into ashes.
13. I can cause the earth to shake.
14. I can erupt suddenly.
15. I cause natural disasters.
16. Mt. Vesuvius and Mt. Fuji are two of me.
17. My name comes from the Roman god of fire.
18. My lava is not a lamp.
19. I was very active when the earth was formed.
20. I can be dangerous.

15

THINGS

I AM A VOLCANO

I AM A THING

1. I love candy corn and pumpkin pie.
2. Orange and black are my colors.
3. I make you wear costumes.
4. I am celebrated at night.
5. I only come once a year.
6. I think it's O.K. to take candy from strangers.
7. I developed from ancient New Years' festivals.
8. I am a holiday.
9. I am not scared of the dark.
10. I like jack-o'-lanterns.
11. My day is October 31.
12. I became popular in the 1800s.
13. I am a good excuse to have a masquerade party.
14. I make people choose between tricks and treats.
15. I finish every October.
16. I increase pumpkin sales.
17. I am a good day for witches and ghosts.
18. I can be a scary day.
19. I love haunted houses.
20. Kids love me.

16

THINGS

I AM HALLOWEEN

I AM A THING

1. You can watch me on TV.
2. I was created by Jim Henson.
3. I have puppets for friends.
4. Bob and Maria live on me.
5. I am a television show.
6. I am home to a big, talking, yellow bird.
7. I am a street.
8. I am home to a guy who lives in a trash can.
9. My monster loves cookies.
10. I can teach you the alphabet.
11. My Dracula knows how to count.
12. Ernie lives on me.
13. I've seen talking frogs and pigs.
14. I am part of Public Television.
15. My theme song asks, "Can you tell me how to get" to me.
16. Little kids love me.
17. I have been around since before you were born.
18. Stars like to stop by.
19. I am fun to watch.
20. I can help you learn arithmetic.

17

THINGS

I AM *SESAME STREET*

I AM A THING

1. I'll take you to higher places.
2. You can't climb me, but you can use me to go up.
3. I'll put a spring in your step.
4. Shoes are not allowed with me.
5. I come in different sizes.
6. My main part is usually black.
7. Kids love me.
8. I make some people feel dizzy.
9. Tigger would probably like me.
10. I'm sometimes kept in the backyard.
11. Gymnasts know me.
12. My tramp doesn't know Lady.
13. I'll make you go up and down and up and down and up and down …
14. Mini versions of me can be found indoors.
15. Gasoline and I have the same ending.
16. If you like jumping, you'll like me.
17. Use your feet to get me going.
18. Tom Hanks played on me in *Big*.
19. I tend to be round.
20. I have more legs than you do.

18

THINGS

I AM A TRAMPOLINE

I AM A THING

1. I am over 100 years old.
2. A broken chain lies at my feet.
3. I am in New York Harbor.
4. I was made by humans.
5. I always have a bible with me.
6. I have a great view of New York City.
7. I wear a loose robe.
8. I am a woman.
9. I hold a tablet that says July 4, 1776.
10. I am 151 feet, 1 inch tall.
11. I hold a torch.
12. You can visit me by ferry.
13. Two stairways run inside me.
14. I wear a crown with seven spikes.
15. I am very independent.
16. If I sat down, I'd get wet.
17. I welcome visitors from out of town before they reach New York Harbor.
18. Two million people visit me yearly.
19. I am a symbol of the US.
20. I was given to the American people by the French.

19

THINGS

I AM THE STATUE OF LIBERTY

I AM A THING

1. I let people glide on wheels.
2. Some people play a kind of hockey on me.
3. I usually have a toe stopper.
4. I liked to be laced up.
5. People use me on sidewalks.
6. Sometimes I have four wheels.
7. Some people wear kneepads when they use me.
8. I was invented in Belgium about 1870.
9. I am made by humans.
10. I am a great source of exercise.
11. You need coordination to use me.
12. You wear me on your feet.
13. With me you move faster than walking.
14. I need a smooth surface.
15. You can buy me in a toy store.
16. Both kids and adults can use me.
17. In a different version of me you can glide on ice.
18. Sometimes I come with a key.
19. I am usually made of leather, metal and plastic.
20. You could use me in rinks or in the park.

20

THINGS

I AM ROLLER SKATES

I AM A THING

1. The movie *Jaws* was about me.
2. I breathe through gills.
3. My skeleton is made of cartilage.
4. I give birth to live babies.
5. I can swim.
6. I can be a hammerhead or a nurse.
7. Surfers fear me.
8. I like the smell of blood.
9. I can be 50 feet long.
10. People are often scared of me.
11. I live in salt water.
12. My babies are called pups.
13. There are almost 400 different types of my kind.
14. Most of my kind are harmless to humans.
15. My favorite food is fresh fish.
16. I can go for months without eating.
17. I have an excellent sense of smell.
18. Most kinds of me have more than four rows of teeth.
19. I am a sea animal.
20. I've been known to eat my own relatives.

21

THINGS

I AM A SHARK

I AM A THING

 1. I hang out at the supermarket.
 2. I am eaten.
 3. I come from South America.
 4. I grow on trees, upside down.
 5. I am a fruit.
 6. Sometimes bread and pancakes are made with me.
 7. Monkeys love me.
 8. Some use my name to say they are nuts.
 9. I come in bunches.
10. A clothing store bears my name.
11. I come with a peel.
12. My name has lots of As but only one B.
13. I can become a famous ice cream treat.
14. I get sweeter as I age.
15. My inside is usually yellow.
16. I can be fried.
17. I can be chocolate and frozen.
18. Some people eat me with cereal.
19. I might have a Chiquita label.
20. I am soft and mushy.

22

THINGS

I AM A BANANA

I AM A THING

1. Kids are nuts about me.
2. I'm good with a glass of milk.
3. I'm pretty gooey.
4. Sometimes I'm chunky.
5. Lots of kids eat me for lunch.
6. I am rectangular in shape.
7. I have no money, but I have bread.
8. I am a food.
9. I'm nutty and fruity.
10. I'm as American as apple pie.
11. I am a kind of sandwich.
12. I can be PB&J for short.
13. I am served cold.
14. I'm made of three food groups.
15. If you cut me, I won't bleed.
16. I might stick to the roof of your mouth.
17. I'm quick to make if you are in a jam.
18. Without bread, I'm not myself.
19. You don't have to cook me to eat me.
20. You can make me in a jiffy.

23

THINGS

I AM A PEANUT BUTTER & JELLY SANDWICH

I AM A THING

1. You can't wear my rings.
2. I'm home to clowns.
3. I travel far and wide.
4. My people fly without airplanes.
5. I can come with a trapeze.
6. No one sleeps in my tent.
7. I often travel by train.
8. I juggle a lot of things at once.
9. P.T. Barnum helped make me popular.
10. I often have three rings.
11. I have sideshows.
12. You can sit in my stands.
13. I serve popcorn and cotton candy.
14. I have a ringmaster.
15. My cats are big.
16. I travel with elephants.
17. I'm "The Greatest Show on Earth."
18. I'm fun for all ages.
19. I might know a bearded lady.
20. I have lots of animals.

24

THINGS

I AM A CIRCUS

I AM A THING

1. I'm not a bird but I can fly.
2. St. George was no friend of mine.
3. If you've read *The Hobbit,* you know me.
4. Zak and Cassie tell my tales on PBS.
5. No amount of lotion will ever cure my scaly skin.
6. When Pete knew me, he called me Elliot.
7. My home is usually called a lair.
8. Role players like dungeons and me.
9. I'm a mythological creature … or am I?
10. Little Jackie Paper brought me strings and sealing wax.
11. I look like a big lizard.
12. I feel right at home in a mountain cave.
13. Legend says that bold knights rescued princesses from my evil clutches.
14. Some say that I'm magic.
15. I've been known to breathe fire.
16. I'm not a wagon but I sound like one.
17. If you've read *Harry Potter*, you know that Charlie Weasley works with my kind in Romania.
18. I have horns and a big tail.
19. This topic is starting to drag on a bit, don't you think?
20. My kind has been known to hoard treasure but we're not pirates.

25

THINGS

I AM A DRAGON